SHIFTING INTO PURPOSE

PURPOSE

The Journey to Entrepreneurship

Raquel M. R. Thomas

ISBN: 1721979484
ISBN 13: 978-1721979486

A DEDICATION TO YOU

This book is dedicated to every person who is struggling with the fear of starting his or her own business. We are often told what we cannot do. What we need to hear more often is what we can do. I am here to tell you that you can and you will, if you are willing to do the work. This is the season of greater! The season of sowing seeds to prepare for your harvest season! It is time to "shift into purpose"!

To my children, Roman and Raquel—you push me to new heights. I thank you for allowing me to be Mommy, provider, protector, and your leader. I love you both, and all that I do is for you and the legacy of our family.

To my Tiny Tubby—thank you for believing in me and encouraging my dream to change the world one individual at a time. Thank you for not only seeing my vision but also being willing to join me in my mission to inspire, create, build, restore, and, most importantly, give hope to the hopeless. Thank you. I love you!

To every reader—know that in your journey, people will doubt you and even speak poorly about you. Stay on your path. Remain grounded in what you know to be true. All things of worth require hard work and what most people see is the completed project. They will not see the late nights, long hours, tears, and your fears. The shift to purpose will not always be easy, but it will always be worth the transition. Never give up on yourself, and when the storm comes, know that all storms will pass; they don't stay. Your "greater" is in your "shift to purpose."

Thank you to everyone who has supported me and poured your positive energy into my movement along the years! Without you, nothing that I do is possible.

CONTENTS

Chapter 1

SHIFTING INTO PURPOSE

The question that I'm often asked is, "How did you start your first business?" The answer is rather simple: I was shifting into my purpose—that is, shifting into the next season of my life. I like to say my time for the greater had come, and I was ready when God called my name. Many are called, but few are chosen. I like to think of myself as one of the chosen. I have always ordered my steps, and, more importantly, I have always had the heart of a winner. In any situation there is never a doubt whether my heart is in the game. The question I ask you is, "Is your heart in the game?" The answer to this question determines if you are ready for the greater.

Shifting into purpose is a journey. In my journey, I knew I wanted to walk in my purpose. Walking in purpose in my entrepreneurial career meant changing lives and inspiring people. I wanted to give hope. As a young girl who grew up in an unstable home without guidance, I wanted to use my story to show people that all things are possible despite our circumstances. I knew I had a story to tell and a legacy to fulfill. All my life I had been preparing to share my story with you all to inspire you on your journey to entrepreneurship.

I will ask you a few questions, all of which I asked myself when I started on my entrepreneurship journey:

1. What is your divine ache?

2. What is your legacy?

3. Are you ready for your shift to greater?

All my answers aligned, and it is how I knew it was time to start my own business. Are your answers aligned?

Chapter 2

THE JAY Z EFFECT AND THE OPRAH EFFECT

In most cases, there is always someone whom we look at and say, "Wow! This girl or guy inspires me to chase my dreams." In some cases, you share some type of commonality with the people who cause the wow effect. For me, that guy was Jay Z. There is no question the rapper and business icon is known around the world for not only his music but also his business savvy. We all know Jay Z had mountains to climb and overcome in his life, but without a doubt, the guy is a winner. So, as a young girl living in poverty, when I saw his success, I knew that I too could succeed beyond my situation. I knew that if I focused on my God-given gifts and stayed within my purpose, I could win, just like Jay Z. I don't know Jay Z, but, I would say from watching his body of work over the years, when his time came to shift from the streets to music and again from music to business, he was ready and aligned with his true purpose.

From the early 1990s to now, Jay Z is still evolving and growing his businesses. From the outside looking in, I decided to fall into the Jay Z effect. For me, the Jay Z effect means never stop shifting and never be afraid to try something new. Opportunities come to those who make moves within their purpose. Doors will open when we work with our God-given gifts and purpose. Find someone who will inspire you to do better. Find someone you find commonality with, because it will give you hope in times of need. Find the person who gives you the wow effect. I also want you to understand that the person does not have to be famous—just a person who inspires you to chase your dreams.

In my teenage years, I found a second person who gave me the wow effect. I'm sure many women and men are inspired by Oprah. When I was bit by the Oprah effect, I knew that being myself was my most powerful tool. Oprah also made me feel, as a young woman, that I could accomplish anything despite my race or gender. Like Oprah, my relationship with my biological mother was strained. Beyond that commonality, we also share the same skin complexion and gender, which gave me an internal power that wasn't visible but was embedded deep within my heart. She gave me hope.

When I think of a winner, I can't think of a more deserving winner, or someone whose work ethic shows in their body of work, than Oprah. Beyond the TV shows and movies, Oprah's work has a purpose. Her philanthropic work and generous donations to, and for, children around the world is inspiring. I strongly believe that Oprah's shift into purpose has been her guiding light. That light has shone brightly on her because her journey in business is with a purpose. Again, find the person who gives you the wow effect. As you journey, it helps to reflect on those who have done the work, which, in turn, will inspire you.

Chapter 3

JOURNEY TO PURPOSE

When we take in our first breath at birth, we enter the world on our journey to purpose. Along the way we may become distracted or delayed, but, ultimately, we get started from the day we take our first breath on our journey to purpose. If this is true, why do some of us never fulfill our purpose? Well, we allow life to happen. We allow our time to be controlled by others and even given up by others. What I have learned in my journey to purpose is that time is the most important determining factor of my life. Time is borrowed, and we can never get it back once it is gone. So, what we do with our time determines if we complete our journey to purpose.

If you are off path, you can get back on the correct path to your purpose. Lessons of trial and tribulations are needed to continue the journey. The knowledge you gain from the lesson will help you in entrepreneurship. The one thing that has always been true for me is that all things work for my good, regardless of it being good or bad. Your journey to purpose is just that—*your journey*—and it may look different from what you expected. Your journey may even be delayed, but you don't need to worry, as your journey will lead you to your purpose. All things happen as they should and in divine order when we work hard.

Chapter 4

PRINCIPLES GUIDING THE SHIFT TO PURPOSE

1. **Protect your energy**
   * Keep the dream killers away from you. These are the people who will cause doubt to seep in your dreams.
   * There will be bad days along the way, but there is always a lesson in the bad days.
   * Always remain positive.
2. **Create your own happiness**
   * What do you need?
   * What do you want?
3. **Enjoy the moment**
   * Be present because you can never get that special moment back once it is gone.
   * Respect the moment.
   * Acknowledge your own successes and celebrate yourself.
4. **Believe in yourself**
   * It starts with *you*.
   * You are the best you.
5. **Keep moving**
   * No matter what happens, don't get stuck.
   * You will get more no's than yeses, but you only need one yes.
   * There will be trials and sacrifices along the way.
   * Learn from the mistakes because they are lessons as well.
6. **Commit to your own process**
   * Follow your business and life plan.
   * Remain open to revisions.

7. **Remain a student**
   * Always position yourself to learn.
   * Utilize your vehicles/drivers; they will take you from point A to point B.
8. **Respect all things before and after you**
   * Past.
   * Present.
   * Future.
9. **Know that you are your best self**
   * Refrain from emulating others.
   * Being you yields the best results.
10. **Become a dream catcher**
    * Once you lock in on the purpose of the vision, move forward with catching the dream.
    * Any dream is possible, but you must be willing to do the work.

"Let us not become weary in doing good, for at the proper time we will reap a harvest if we do not give up" (Galatians 6:9).

Chapter 5

ENTREPRENEURSHIP WITH PURPOSE

We have discussed shifting into purpose, the Jay Z effect and the Oprah effect, the journey to purpose, and the ten principles that have guided the shift to my purpose. Now, we move on to becoming an entrepreneur with purpose. My journey to entrepreneurship has all been about purpose. Very similar to building blocks, to get to a higher place, you must build one block on top of the other, one block at a time. For me it started with a commercial janitorial business. To answer your question, no, I didn't see cleaning buildings as my purpose, but it led me to my purpose. I started this business first because I wanted to gain experience in entrepreneurship. I had done the research and knew the start-up cost. I knew the overhead costs would not be expensive. It was a great starter business, and I could see what I was capable of. This business taught me many lessons, and it also sharpened my entrepreneurial mind. How? Well, it taught me how to negotiate contracts, how to order inventory, communication techniques, work ethic, and punctuality. More importantly, I could fully understand why time management is key to having a successful business. This business started very small, with cleaning residential homes, and within one year, we had our first commercial contract. The purpose of the cleaning business was to teach me how to run my forthcoming businesses of purpose.

After two years of the cleaning business, I started to shift. My mind-set was shifting into a direction of purpose—a direction of divine purpose. I had learned the tools needed to run a small business from my first business, but I knew I was not working in my purpose. One day I was driving my car, and I started to think of doing work that would give me happiness. By now, I'm walking into year three of the cleaning business. My firstborn was with me all the time. We were approaching the time in which we needed to put him in daycare. The daycare search was no fun because I couldn't seem to find a place that pleased me 100 percent. Then it hit me. I was no longer working my corporate job, and I was only running my cleaning business. So, I decided to take a house that I owned, and I turned it into the daycare center I saw fit for my son. My happiness was found in being with my son and teaching him. I found no greater joy than teaching him. I was working in my true purpose and that purpose was layered. I was working with my son—whom I loved dearly—I was educating him, and I was happy. I launched my second business, which was childcare. In childcare, I could educate and soak in all the joy of being around children. When I opened the doors to my first daycare learning center, I knew I was working in my purpose, and my journey to entrepreneurship with purpose was beginning.

For me, entrepreneurship with purpose meant working within my gifts. I started using what was in my hands and in my heart. Each business after that tied directly into my purpose. Everything I did from that point forward was in my purpose. I knew that if my journey was with a purpose, I would always find happiness in my work even on the bad and difficult days. My purpose became clearer each day, week, and year. I started to teach beyond the daycare centers. I started sharing my life story, and before I knew it, I was in the business of saving lives by inspiring, creating hope, and teaching entrepreneurship with purpose.

In chapter 1, I asked you three questions. It is now time to answer those questions in addition to one more question.

1. What are your gifts and talents?

2. What is your divine ache?

3. What is your legacy?

4. Are you ready for your shift to the greater?

Thus far I have shared with you my shift into purpose and my journey to entrepreneurship with purpose. The next chapters are solely about entrepreneurship and building your business, that is, what you need to know to get started.

ENTREPRENEURSHIP TRAINING GUIDE

A. PRETEST

Let's see what you already know! Don't worry about what you don't know. You will know what is necessary to start your own business by the time you are done with this workbook!

Complete the pretest below:

Circle or use the lines provided to answer the following questions.

1. **TRUE or FALSE**. When starting a business, only new business owners should have a checklist to assist with opening a business.

2. What is your supply?

   _____

   _____

   _____

3. **TRUE or FALSE**. It is important to know your competitors.

4. **TRUE or FALSE**. Not knowing your competitors' price will not affect your business.

5. Why is the location of your business important?

_____

_____

_____

6. Which type of business has a lower overhead?

_____

_____

_____

7. **TRUE or FALSE**. There is no benefit in having an online store.

8. What is a SWOT analysis?

_____

_____

_____

9. **TRUE or FALSE**. Every business should have a business plan to acquire a loan, leasing a space for your business, and to have your plan in writing for reference as an organizing tool.

10. **TRUE or FALSE**. The only way to promote a business is through social media.

11. Name three financing options.

_____

_____

_____

12. **TRUE or FALSE**. The most common type of business entity is a limited liability company, more commonly called an LLC.

13. Why is it important to verify the name of your business with the secretary of state?

_____

_____

_____

14. **TRUE or FALSE.** You can use the name of an existing business.

15. What is a FEIN?

   _____

   _____

   _____

16. **TRUE or FALSE.** A D-U-N-S number is mandatory to obtain federal government contracts and grants.

17. Where can you find out in your state what type of license is needed for your business?

   _____

   _____

   _____

18. **TRUE or FALSE.** Having a logo for your business is very important to your business and is needed to effectively market and brand your business.

19. What does a trademark guarantee the owner?

   _____

   _____

   _____

20. What is a copyright?

   _____

   _____

   _____

21. What are the three types of patents?

   _____

   _____

   _____

22. **TRUE or FALSE.** A business needs business insurance to protect it from different types of risks that the business could face.

23. What does general liability insurance cover?

_____

_____

_____

24. What does workers compensation insurance cover?

_____

_____

_____

25. What are the four steps used to hire a strong staff?

_____

_____

_____

26. **TRUE or FALSE**. Having an accountant is not mandatory to operate your business.

27. **TRUE or FALSE**. Taxes are the same in each state.

28. How often are income taxes normally filed?

_____

_____

_____

29. Whom should you hire to do your taxes for your business?

_____

_____

_____

30. **TRUE or FALSE**. There are no penalties when you do not pay your taxes.

B. BUSINESS CHECKLIST

My suggestion to beginners and experienced business owners is to always create a checklist. It's your map to success. There is beauty in being able to map out your journey! You must create a flexible checklist that can be adjusted for your business. Below is a checklist that will be helpful along the journey.

1. ASSESSING YOUR PURPOSE AND GIFTS

- ❏ Determine your why
- ❏ Complete a SWOT analysis to identify your strengths and weaknesses
- ❏ Determine if you will have a product or a service; build an online business or physical location
- ❏ Make a list of business ideas that fit your strengths and interests
- ❏ Identify businesses that are successful today
- ❏ Understand the problem(s) your business will solve
- ❏ Define the market you want to pursue and determine your target customer

2. SETTING UP YOUR BUSINESS

- ❏ Conduct a financial assessment
- ❏ Select your business name and search the Internet to make sure it's not being used
- ❏ Register a domain name and secure social-media profiles for the company
- ❏ Apply for a EIN with the IRS and local or state business licenses
- ❏ Decide on a legal structure or business structure and incorporate: corporation, LLC, or sole proprietorship
- ❏ Develop an operating website
- ❏ Evaluate and select needed insurance policies for your business: liability, workers comp, and/or health insurance
- ❏ Open a business bank account and have a business credit card(s)
- ❏ Begin networking with premarketing materials, such as business cards, brochures, or public relations

3. PLANNING FOR YOUR BUSINESS

- ❏ Write an executive summary after the other sections of the business plan are completed below
- ❏ Complete a company overview that includes basic information and a summary of the management team
- ❏ Write a product description section describing your products or services and what problems they solve Describe an operating plan for the business, such as operating hours, number of employees, key suppliers, or seasonal adjustments your business might need to adjust to
- ❏ Create a marketing and sales plan that includes a go-to market or launch plan, pricing, how your business will generate leads, and close new business
- ❏ Build a financial plan that shows a break-even analysis, projected profit and loss, and projected cash flows

4. MARKETING AND BRANDING YOUR BUSINESS

- ❏ Develop a brand for your company
- ❏ Distribute or display your marketing materials: shop signs, brochures, or banners
- ❏ Initiate digital marketing through blogs, e-mails, or SEO strategies to drive traffic to your website
- ❏ Contact your local or regional press
- ❏ Organize a grand opening day

C. SUPPLY AND DEMAND

One of the most important questions you must ask yourself during this phase is, "Will the consumer want my product or service? Is my product or service needed in the marketplace?" Supply and demand is the amount of a product that is available and the amount that is wanted by consumers. The demand of your supply will be determined by the desire of the consumer. The key to supply and demand is price. Are you properly priced in the marketplace? Market research must be completed. It is important to learn what your competitors are selling their supply for. Once your supply is properly priced, you will be able to determine your demand. You do not want to price yourself out of the market, nor do you want to price your supply below market value. I like to call the placement of price point the "sweet spot." What is the sweet spot in your marketplace? A great problem to have is not meeting the demand, but a bad problem to have is not having any demand for your product or supply. You must properly place yourself in the marketplace for success.

1. What is your supply?

2. What is the price of your supply?

3. Who are your competitors, and what are their prices?

D. LOCATION OF BUSINESS

Once you have determined exactly what you are selling to the consumer, you will need to decide where you will sell your product or service. Many small businesses start their businesses online first because it lowers the overhead cost. An online business enables the consumer to find, order, and pay for products and services through a website. Online businesses are growing rapidly and are becoming more convenient for the consumer.

In some cases, the business will move directly into a brick-and-mortar (or storefront). A brick-and-mortar store or office is used to differentiate the businesses that operate from built-up properties or storefronts from those that operate entirely from their websites. In some cases, a brick-and-mortar may serve your consumer better. You will need to assess your consumers and their wants to determine what will be best for your business.

1. Where will you locate your business?

2. What are the benefits of having an online store versus a brick-and-mortar?

3. What are the benefits of having a brick-and-mortar versus an online store?

E. CREATING A BUSINESS PLAN AND BUDGET

In my experience with some of my businesses, I had to provide a business plan that showed how I was going to operate and, more importantly, be a profitable business. If you find yourself asking for a business loan from a bank, do not consider going without a business plan. When asking a bank for a loan, one of the most important pieces to the puzzle is showing them your business plan. Beyond your business plan, you will need to show that your business is able to survive and make money to repay the loan! Getting a loan is no easy task, even with a business plan. Nevertheless, show up prepared to present your idea in writing. In the event you don't need a business loan or need to provide the business plan for another person, you will need a business plan for yourself. A good rule of thumb is to always have a business plan.

The major components of a business plan are listed below but can vary:

TITLE PAGE

The title page is for your name and the name of your business.

EXECUTIVE SUMMARY

The executive summary should be written last, although it will be the leading piece of your business plan. It should not be more than one page and should highlight your business at a high level.

BUSINESS DESCRIPTION

The business description is a summary or overview of your business, including what product or service you will provide, a detailed description of the product, your mission and vision for the business, the management team, the legal structure and ownership, and the location of your business.

MARKET ANALYSIS

The market analysis will explain your understanding of the market that you will service. It will also provide an overview of the industry that your business will participate in. You should also give a detailed description of the target market, geographic location, demographics, buyer characteristics, and your target market's needs.

COMPETITIVE ANALYSIS AND SWOT ANALYSIS

The competitive analysis lays out the businesses you are competing with and against. When identifying the competition, you should identify how your voice will be heard over the noise of competitors.

The competitive analysis should reflect how your business is different from and better than your competition.

The SWOT analysis is one of the best tools you can use to help guide you as you build your business and marketing campaign. The SWOT analysis will reflect the **S**trengths, **W**eaknesses, **O**pportunities, and **T**hreats that you will face on your entrepreneurial journey.

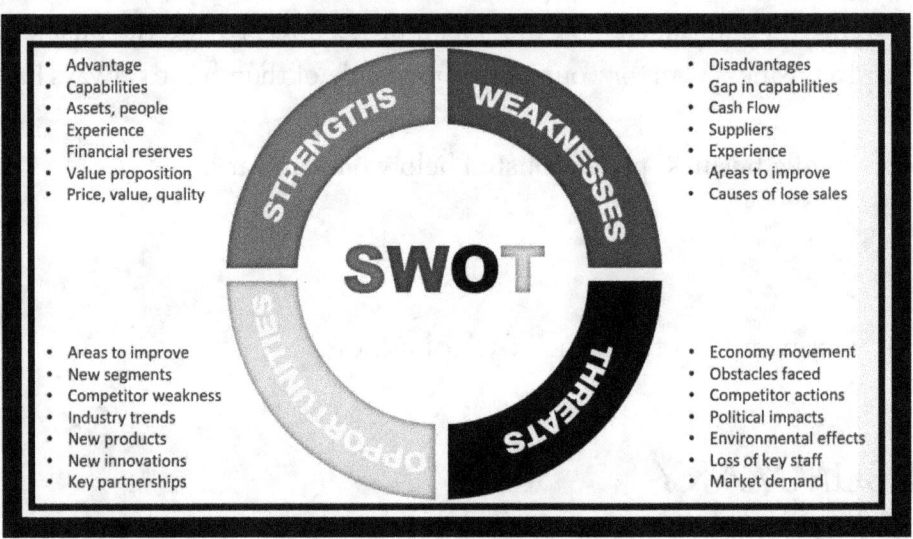

MANAGEMENT

The management team will need to be identified. It is important to explain who will run your business and that person's experience. You should also highlight the role of the manager and employees for the business. An organizational chart is a great tool to add to this section of your business plan, and depending on your business, a short bio would be a good addition.

MARKETING AND BRANDING

Now the fun part of your journey! In the marketing and branding section of your business plan, you will need to explain your plan for consumer engagement with your business. There is a difference between marketing and branding, and it is very important to know that difference. Marketing is how you move from concept to the consumer. Branding is creating a unique name and image that the consumer associates with your product or service. Promotion is the most important function of any business. There are many promotion options:

* Social media digital marketing (Facebook, Twitter, Instagram, LinkedIn)
* Media advertising (newspaper, magazine, television, radio)

* Direct mail
* Seminars or business conferences
* Joint advertising with other companies
* Word of mouth or fixed signage

FINANCIAL PLAN AND BUDGET

Creating a financial plan and budget is where all the business planning truly comes together. You must know your expenses because they will impact your entire business. A comprehensive financial plan will also give you a baseline for your profit margin. There are two spreadsheets below that you can use as a guide to determine your projected startup costs and your projected profit and loss.

* **Projected Start-Up Costs:** One-time-cost items that you might need to open your business.
* **Projected Profit and Loss:** A twelve-month forecast for your business that shows your projected sales and gross profit.

ESTIMATED START-UP COST

START-UP COST				
				Date:
COST ITEMS	MONTHS	COST/MONTH	ONE-TIME COST	TOTAL COST
Marketing				$0
Salaries				$0
Employee Payroll Taxes				$0
Rent and Utilities				$0
Postage				$0
Telephone				$0
Computer Equipment				$0
Computer Software				$0
Insurance				$0
Interest Expense				$0
Bank Service Charges				$0
Office Supplies				$0
Travel & Entertainment				$0
Equipment				$0
Furniture & Fixtures				$0
Improvements				$0
Donations				$0
Business Licenses and Permits				$0
Professional Services				$0
Consultant(s)				$0
Inventory				$0
Cash on Hand (Working Capital)				$0
Miscellaneous				$0
ESTIMATED START-UP BUDGET				$0

PROJECTED PROFIT-AND-LOSS START-UP COSTS

START-UP COST

Date:

REVENUE	JAN	FEB	MAR	APR	MAY	JUN	JUL	AUG	SEP	OCT	NOV	DEC	YTD
Estimated Product Sales	$0	$0	$0	$0	$0	$0	$0	$0	$0	$0	$0	$0	$0
Returns & Discounts	$0	$0	$0	$0	$0	$0	$0	$0	$0	$0	$0	$0	$0
Service Revenue	$0	$0	$0	$0	$0	$0	$0	$0	$0	$0	$0	$0	$0
Other Revenue	$0	$0	$0	$0	$0	$0	$0	$0	$0	$0	$0	$0	$0
Net Sales	$0	$0	$0	$0	$0	$0	$0	$0	$0	$0	$0	$0	$0
Cost of Goods Sold	$0	$0	$0	$0	$0	$0	$0	$0	$0	$0	$0	$0	$0
Gross Profit	$0	$0	$0	$0	$0	$0	$0	$0	$0	$0	$0	$0	$0

EXPENSES	JAN	FEB	MAR	APR	MAY	JUN	JUL	AUG	SEP	OCT	NOV	DEC	YTD
Salaries & Wages	$0	$0	$0	$0	$0	$0	$0	$0	$0	$0	$0	$0	$0
Marketing	$0	$0	$0	$0	$0	$0	$0	$0	$0	$0	$0	$0	$0
Sales Commissions	$0	$0	$0	$0	$0	$0	$0	$0	$0	$0	$0	$0	$0
Rent	$0	$0	$0	$0	$0	$0	$0	$0	$0	$0	$0	$0	$0
Utilities	$0	$0	$0	$0	$0	$0	$0	$0	$0	$0	$0	$0	$0
Website Expenses	$0	$0	$0	$0	$0	$0	$0	$0	$0	$0	$0	$0	$0
Internet/Phone	$0	$0	$0	$0	$0	$0	$0	$0	$0	$0	$0	$0	$0
Insurance	$0	$0	$0	$0	$0	$0	$0	$0	$0	$0	$0	$0	$0
Travel	$0	$0	$0	$0	$0	$0	$0	$0	$0	$0	$0	$0	$0
Legal/Accounting	$0	$0	$0	$0	$0	$0	$0	$0	$0	$0	$0	$0	$0
Office Supplies	$0	$0	$0	$0	$0	$0	$0	$0	$0	$0	$0	$0	$0
Interest Expense	$0	$0	$0	$0	$0	$0	$0	$0	$0	$0	$0	$0	$0
Other 1	$0	$0	$0	$0	$0	$0	$0	$0	$0	$0	$0	$0	$0
Total Expenses													$0
Income Before Taxes													$0
Income-Tax Expense													

NET INCOME													

F. FINANCING YOUR BUSINESS

How will you finance your business? Personally, I believe it is important to be able to invest in yourself first before ever asking for someone else to invest in your dream. The question I asked myself is how important is this to me?. That answer determines if you are willing to sacrifice your own money. When we use our own finances, we work harder; this is not to say we don't work hard when we use other investments. With that said, there are other options that many business owners use to finance their business. The options include, but are not limited to, the following:

1. Personal capital
2. Family and friends
3. Loan
4. Capital investors
5. Grants
6. Fundraisers

Now that you have financing options, which option(s) would you select and why?

G. BUSINESS STRUCTURE

Be careful of creating a sole proprietorship as your business structure. Sole proprietorship is a type of business structure that holds you, the owner of the business, personally liable for all financial obligations and debt. Sole proprietorship is the most common business structure model.

The second most common type of business entity is a limited liability company, more commonly referenced as an LLC. LLC is a corporate structure in which the members cannot be held personally liable for the company's debt. My recommendation for a new business owner would be to create an LLC.

There are other business entities, including corporations, partnerships, and nonprofit organizations. Each entity has its perks, but it is up to you to determine what will best fit your business. Assess the advantages and disadvantages of each business entity along with the tax structure of each one to determine which will work best for your type of business.

1. What is an LLC?

2. What is sole proprietorship?

H. BUSINESS NAME

Most of us have a name for our business before we have a business plan, and that's OK! However, when it is time to register your business, you will need to do a name search in the state in which you will incorporate your business. Each state has a website that can be used to verify if the name that you have selected is available. In most states you can go to the secretary of state website to complete a name search. This is a commonly used tool for each state. Once you have typed in the name of your choice, the system will check and advise if the name is available or not.

In some instances, another business may already have the name you wanted for your business. If the name you want is already being utilized, you will need to select a different name for your business. This search is very important to do in the early stages so you have time to adjust if necessary. You can make minor changes in the name if you are fixated on a particular name. You may be able to adjust the spelling or punctuation in the name to make it different. If there is some difference in the name, and no one else is using the same name, you can use it.

Your business name is very important and will become your largest marketing and branding tool. Your goal is to make your business name a household name in your community and widely known. So be very mindful when selecting your business name. Make sure it is something you will still love twenty years from now!

Once you have selected your name, you must register your business with the governing state of your business. To register your business as an LLC, partnership, or sole proprietorship, you will need to go to the secretary of state website to apply using your selected business name. There are also third-party companies that you will have the opportunity to pay to set up your business entity if you do not feel comfortable doing it yourself.

1. Why is it important to verify the name of your business with the secretary of state?

2. What can you do if your business name already exists?

I. REGISTER YOUR BUSINESS

Now that you have a business name and have filed for your business, it is time to acquire your Federal Employer Identification Number, commonly called FEIN or EIN. The EIN is a nine-digit unique number assigned by the Internal Revenue Service (IRS) for businesses operating in the United States. The identification number is used for all business accounts and is an identifying marker beyond your business name. You cannot receive a business banking account without an EIN. Your EIN is very similar to your social security number, and the IRS uses it to track your tax return. Yes, your business will need to file taxes yearly. In later modules you will learn more about the different taxes businesses are required to file and pay.

I would encourage all businesses to acquire a Dun & Bradstreet D-U-N-S number. The D-U-N-S number is how your business credit is tracked and scored. Like your social security number and your EIN, the D-U-N-S number also has nine digits. The D-U-N-S number is required to register for any U.S. federal government contract or grant.

You will also need to acquire any licenses required by the state in which your business is registered. Common licenses are sales and use tax license, general business license, retail license, and resale license. License information is also commonly found on the secretary of state website. To legally operate your business, you will need the proper licenses. Licenses can and will vary depending on the state where your business is registered.

1. What is a FEIN and why is it needed?

2. What is a D-U-N-S number and why is it needed?

3. Where can you find out in your state what type of license is needed for your business?

J. LOGO

For any business you will need a logo. A logo is a recognizable and distinctive graphic design that identifies your business. When branded properly, your logo should automatically be associated with your business name and vice versa.

Trademark is a form of insurance, and you should trademark your logo. A trademark guarantees that your logo keeps its genuineness and gives the business owner the legal rights to prevent unauthorized use of the trademark. A service mark is very similar to a trademark, but the service mark distinguishes services versus a product. What does this mean? If another company or person uses your logo design, and you have legally trademarked your design, you have the legal power to have that company or person remove the logo from their business and/or event. A federal trademark is good for ten years and can be renewed after ten years.

Copyrights are similar to trademarks for written materials. A copyright protects published or unpublished original work for fifty years beyond the life of the person who created the work. An example of an original work would be a published book by an author. The book is covered under the copyright for the life of the author and fifty years after the author's death. A work can be duplicated without due credit after this time and does not require a payment to the original author.

Patents protect an invention; it prohibits someone else from copying the same invention. A patent can be granted by the U.S. Patent and Trademark Office. The term for a patent is twenty years from the date it was filed.

There are three types of patents: utility patent, design patent, and plant patent.

A **utility patent** covers a creation of a new or improved service, product, or machine.

A **design patent** protects you as the inventor by prohibiting others from using the original shape and ornamentation of your functional design.

A not-so-common patent is the **plant patent**. It is an asexually reproduced plant that isn't a tuber propagate plant or found in an uncultivated state.

1. Why should your business have a logo?

2. What does a trademark guarantee the owner?

3. What is a copyright?

4. What are the three types of patents?

K. INSURANCE

Insurance is necessary for most businesses. The most common insurance is general liability insurance. General liability insurance, which is also referred to as business liability insurance, protects the business from property, bodily injury, and personal injury claims against the business.

Workers compensation insurance is another commonly used insurance in business. Workers compensation is a state-mandated insurance to cover lost wages and medical treatment due to a work-related injury or illness. Many of us may know someone who has been hurt on their job and they still receive pay; those individuals are being paid from workers compensation insurance versus a traditional payroll.

Another common insurance type is commercial vehicle insurance. Commercial vehicle insurance is for businesses that use vehicles for their business. Commercial vehicle insurance is more expensive than personal vehicle insurance because there is typically more risk associated with commercial vehicles. Research the companies offering this type of insurance because you want to be fully informed of the coverage details, liability limits, and the rules and regulations that you may have to meet for your type of business.

1. Why is business insurance necessary?

2. What does general liability insurance cover?

3. What does workers compensation insurance cover?

L. HIRING AND BUILDING YOUR TEAM

One of the most important pieces to running a successful business is hiring the correct staff—a staff of individuals who understand your goals and vision for your business. Most small business entrepreneurs will agree that finding good employees who want to work is a task. Many businesses struggle with finding the right employees for their overall business growth. When building a team of managers and employees, there are a few things that should be done in the hiring process. The process will assist you with narrowing down the applicants and by sieving the applications to select the best fit for your company. There are steps that I follow in hiring employees, and these steps do not have to be in this exact order, but, nonetheless, these are the steps that I follow when hiring staff:

Step 1: Résumé and application review
Step 2: Vetting process—calling references and pulling background checks
Step 3: Completing a face-to-face interview (there could be multiple interviews)
Step 4: Having the staff sign a confidentiality and noncompete agreement to protect your business and ideas of the business

While these steps will help you hire and build a strong team, it does not guarantee that they will be the best employees for your company. The only true measure of knowing if you have hired the right staff members is seeing and watching their work habits and efforts. So, while having a solid hiring process in place, you still cannot be 100 percent certain until the manager or employee has shown their work ability.

1. Why is it important to have a hiring process?

M. TAXES

This section will tell you why you need an accountant to assist you with your business. Every business pays taxes, and there are different types of taxes that will need to be paid. In most cases, if you have an accountant, they are going to ensure you are current on your taxes as well as make sure your books are done correctly. Keeping the books simply means keeping track of your income and expenses. Accurate accounting will help you estimate the taxes you owe to the state and federal government. I would recommend that a company review their books with their accountant monthly but never go beyond a quarterly review. While it is your accountant's job to make sure your taxes are being paid and your income and expenses align, it is ultimately your job as the business owner to be knowledgeable about the taxes and laws that govern your company. What is important to know and be aware of is, there are penalties and additional fees when you pay your taxes late or you do not pay at all.

COMMON TAXES THAT ARE PAID:

Income taxes are for both individuals and businesses. Income tax is determined by the product of a tax rate times the taxable income. Simply stated, you are taxed on your income minus your expenses to operate the company. Income taxes for a business are normally filed on March 15th yearly. There are exceptions to this that your accountant should be aware of and will advise you accordingly based on your business.

Sales and use tax is paid monthly or quarterly in most states. This tax is determined by each individual state and their tax rate on the items you have sold. Based on the income made from items sold, you will be taxed a percentage of that amount. For example, if you have a candy store, and your store sold $1,000 in candy sales, your state charges 10 percent tax on the $1,000. You will owe the state $100 in sales and use tax.

If you pay employees, you will have payroll taxes. Payroll taxes are for employers and employees, which are calculated as a percentage of the salaries that the employer pays their hired staff. To be safe and properly represented when completing your payroll taxes, you need an accountant, because taxes vary every payroll. An accountant specializes in this area; ensure that this task is delegated accordingly in your business. It also provides the best protection to you as a business owner.

1. Whom should you hire to complete your taxes and why?

2. How often are income taxes filed?

N. POST-TEST

Circle or use the lines provided to answer the following questions.

1. **TRUE or FALSE**. When starting a business, only new business owners should have a checklist to assist with opening a business.

2. What is your supply?

   _____

   _____

   _____

3. **TRUE or FALSE**. It is important to know your competitors.

4. **TRUE or FALSE**. If you don't know your competitors' price, it will not affect your business.

5. Why is the location of your business important?

   _____

   _____

   _____

6. Which type of business has a lower overhead?

   _____

   _____

   _____

7. **TRUE or FALSE**. There is no benefit of not having an online store.

8. What is a SWOT analysis?

   _____

   _____

   _____

9. **TRUE or FALSE**. Every business should have a business plan to acquire a loan, leasing a space for your business, and to have your plan in writing for reference as an organizing tool.

10. **TRUE or FALSE**. The only way to promote a business is through social media.

11. Name three financing options.

_____

_____

_____

12. **TRUE or FALSE**. The most common type of business entity is a limited liability company, more commonly called an LLC.

13. Why is it important to verify the name of your business with the secretary of state?

_____

_____

_____

14. **TRUE or FALSE**. You can use a name of an existing business name.

15. What is a FEIN?

_____

_____

_____

16. **TRUE or FALSE**. A D-U-N-S number is mandatory to obtain federal government contracts and grants.

17. Where can you find out in your state what type of license is needed for your business?

_____

_____

_____

18. **TRUE or FALSE**. Having a logo for your business is very important to your business and is needed to effectively market and brand your business.

_____

_____

_____

19. What does a trademark guarantee the owner?

_____

_____

_____

20. What is a copyright?

_____

_____

_____

21. What are the three types of patents?

_____

_____

_____

22. **TRUE or FALSE**. A business needs business insurance to protect itself from different types of risks that the business could face.

23. What does general liability insurance cover?

_____

_____

_____

24. What does workers compensation insurance cover?

_____

_____

_____

25. What are the four steps used to hire a strong staff?

_____

_____

_____

26. **TRUE or FALSE.** Having an accountant is not mandatory to operate your business.

27. **TRUE or FALSE.** Taxes are the same in each state.

28. How often are income taxes normally filed?

_____

_____

_____

29. Whom should you hire to do your taxes for your business?

_____

_____

_____

30. **TRUE or FALSE.** There are no penalties when you do not pay your taxes.

BUSINESS KEY TERMS

Balance sheet

A condensed statement that shows the financial position of an entity on a specified date (usually the last day of an accounting period).

Branding

The process involved in creating a unique name and image for a product in the consumers' mind, mainly through advertising campaigns with a consistent theme.

Brick-and-mortar

This term is used to differentiate the businesses that operate from built-up properties or storefronts from those that operate entirely (or almost entirely) from their websites.

Budget

An estimate of costs, revenues, and resources over a specified period, reflecting a reading of future financial conditions and goals.

Business license

A permit to operate an enterprise that is typically required by a government authority before operation commences.

Business plan

Set of documents prepared by a firm's management to summarize its operational and financial objectives for the near future (usually one to three years) and to show how they will be achieved.

Capital

Wealth in the form of money or assets, taken as a sign of the financial strength of an individual, organization, or nation, and assumed to be available for development or investment.

Commercial vehicle insurance

Insurance for businesses that have vehicles that are used for their business purposes; the insurance covers liability and physical damage protection.

Consumer

Purchaser of a good or service in retail.

Copyright

Legal monopoly that protects published or unpublished original work (for the duration of its author's life plus fifty years) from unauthorized duplication without due credit and compensation.

Corporation

Firm that meets certain legal requirements to be recognized as having a legal existence, as an entity separate and distinct from its owners.

Design patent

Protects you as the inventor by prohibiting others from using the original shape ornamentation of your functional design.

Dun & Bradstreet D-U-N-S number

Required to register for any U.S. federal government contract or grant; the number in which your business credit score is accumulated.

FEIN

Acronym for Federal Employer Identification Number. This is a nine-digit unique number assigned by the Internal Revenue Service (IRS) to businesses operating in the United States.

Financial statement

Summary report that shows how a firm has used the funds entrusted to it by its stockholders (shareholders) and lenders and what is its current financial position.

Financing

The act of providing money for a project.

Fundraising
The process of soliciting financial support (usually as grants) for a noncommercial cause.

General liability insurance
Protects the business from property, bodily injury, and personal injury claims against the business.

Grants
Bounty, contribution, gift, or subsidy (in cash or kind) bestowed by a government or other organization (called the grantor) for specified purposes to an eligible recipient (called the grantee).

Hiring
The practice of finding, evaluating, and establishing a working relationship with future employees, interns, contractors, or consultants.

Insurance
Risk-transfer mechanism that ensures full or partial financial compensation for the loss or damage caused by event(s) beyond the control of the insured party.

Investment
Money committed or property acquired for future income.

Investor
Neither a speculator (who takes on high risks for high rewards) nor a gambler (who takes on the risk of total loss for out-of-proportion rewards) but one whose primary objectives are preservation of the original investment (the principal), a steady income, and capital appreciation.

Limited Liability Company (LLC)
Corporate structure that the members cannot be held personally liable for the company's debt.

Loan
Written or oral agreement for a temporary transfer of a property (usually cash) from its owner (the lender) to a borrower, who promises to return it according to the terms of the agreement, usually with interest for its use.

Logo
Recognizable and distinctive graphic design, stylized name, unique symbol, or other device for identifying an organization.

Marketing
The management process through which goods and services move from concept to the customer.

Market research
Component of marketing research whereby a specific market is identified and its size and other characteristics are measured.

Online store
A website that enables visitors to find, order, and pay for products and services.

Overhead
Resource consumed or lost in completing a process that does not contribute directly to the end product.

Partnership
A type of business organization in which two or more individuals pool money, skills, and other resources, and share profit and loss in accordance with terms of the partnership agreement.

Patent
Limited legal monopoly granted to an individual or a firm to make, use, and sell its invention and to exclude others from doing so.

Plant patent
An asexually reproduced plant that isn't a tuber propagate plant or found in an uncultivated state.

Price point
Suggested retail price of a product, determined in such a way as to compete with prices of other products.

Product
A good, idea, method, information, object, or service created as a result of a process and serves a need or satisfies a want.

Profit-and-loss statement
A financial statement that summarizes the revenues, costs, and expenses incurred during a specific period of time, usually a fiscal quarter or year.

Service
Valuable action, deed, or effort performed to satisfy a need or to fulfill a demand.

Service mark

Distinguishes services from a product of a design, graphics, logo, symbols, words, or any combination thereof that uniquely identifies a firm and/or its goods or services, guarantees the item's genuineness, and gives its owner the legal rights to prevent the trademark's unauthorized use.

Small business

Firms of a certain size that fall below certain criteria (that varies from country to country) in terms of annual turnover, number of employees, total value of assets, and so on.

Sole proprietorship

Simplest, oldest, and most common form of business ownership in which only one individual has all the benefits and risks of running an enterprise.

Supply and demand

The amount of a product that is available and the amount that customers want.

SWOT analysis

Situation analysis in which internal strengths and weaknesses of an organization and external opportunities and threats faced by it are closely examined to chart a strategy. SWOT stands for strengths, weaknesses, opportunities, and threats.

Taxes

Compulsory monetary contribution to the state's revenue, assessed and imposed by a government on the activities, enjoyment, expenditure, income, occupation, privilege, property, and so on of individuals and organizations.

Trademark

Distinctive design, graphics, logo, symbols, words, or any combination thereof that uniquely identifies a firm and/or its goods or services, guarantees the item's genuineness, and gives its owner the legal rights to prevent the trademark's unauthorized use.

Utility patent

Covers a creation of a new or improved service, product, or machine.

Workers compensation insurance

State-mandated insurance to cover lost wages and medical treatment due to a work-related injury or illness.

Appendix B

CITATIONS

http://www.businessdictionary.com/
http://www.emarketingdictionary.com/
https://www.entrepreneur.com/
https://www.investopedia.com/
https://www.patriotsoftware.com/
https://www.uspto.gov

Appendix C

ANSWER KEY

1. False. All business owners should use a checklist.
2. Supply is what you are selling.
3. True.
4. False. You must know your competitors' price to remain competitive in the marketplace and gauge what the customer is willing to pay for your product or service.
5. Location is important for various reasons: foot traffic, established businesses near your location, easy access, and so on.
6. Online store.
7. False. Online store has great benefit because of its less overhead costs and less business and personal liability, and you can reach the entire world online.
8. Strengths, weaknesses, opportunities, threats.
9. True.
10. False. There are many ways to promote a business: media advertising (newspaper, magazine, television, radio), direct mail, seminars or business conferences, joint advertising with other companies, and word of mouth or fixed signage.
11. Personal capital, family and friends, loan, capital investors, grants, fundraisers.
12. False. LLC is the second most common, and sole proprietor is the most common.
13. It is important to verify your name with the secretary of state because another company could possibly have the name you want to incorporate.
14. False. You cannot use an existing name legally in the same state in which it is already being used.
15. Federal Employer Identification Number.
16. True.
17. Secretary of state.
18. True.
19. Legal right to use the logo for marketing.

20. A copyright is a legal monopoly that protects published or unpublished original work (for the duration of its author's life plus fifty years) from unauthorized duplication without due credit and compensation.

21. Utility patent, design patent, and plant patent.

22. True.

23. Property, bodily, and personal injury claims against the business.

24. Lost wages and medical treatment due to work-related injury or illness.

25. (1) Résumé and application review (2) Vetting process (3) Face-to-face interview (4) Sign confidentiality and noncompete agreement.

26. True.

27. False. Tax rates vary from state to state.

28. Yearly.

29. Accountant.

30. False. There are penalties and fees that a business will have to pay if taxes are not paid.

AUTHOR BIOGRAPHY

Raquel M. R. Thomas is a writer and business owner from Columbia, South Carolina. A mother of two children, she believes in the value of education and hard work. She strives to demonstrate those values to young people. *Shifting into Purpose: The Journey to Entrepreneurship* is Raquel's second published book, and it was created to provide an outline that she has followed time and time again in her entrepreneurial journey.

Raquel uses her success and achievements to help those just like her—those who may not have the support, resources, or education but possess the drive and vision to see beyond their circumstances. Raquel believed even as a child that she could bring her youthful musings to life—her life! *Shifting into Purpose: The Journey to Entrepreneurship* is a business educational book and workbook designed to be a guiding tool for entrepreneurs who need assistance with the things that are not commonly spoken about in business. This book is the outcome of Raquel's realization that her purpose is to give back and that her early desire is to become a writer. Now, the writings of a troubled second-grader will inspire and motivate the masses.

www.ingramcontent.com/pod-product-compliance
Lightning Source LLC
Chambersburg PA
CBHW081642220526
45468CB00009B/2530